MW00561612

[...]

ALSO BY FADY JOUDAH

Tethered to Stars
Footnotes in the Order of Disappearance
Textu
Alight
The Earth in the Attic

TRANSLATED BY FADY JOUDAH

The Blue Light by Hussein Barghouthi
You Can Be the Last Leaf by Maya Abu Al-Hayyat
The Silence That Remains by Ghassan Zaqtan
with Khaled Mattawa: *A Map of Signs and Scents* by Amjad Nasser
Like a Straw Bird It Follows Me by Ghassan Zaqtan
If I Were Another by Mahmoud Darwish
The Butterfly's Burden by Mahmoud Darwish

[...]

FADY JOUDAH

فادي جودة

MILKWEED EDITIONS

(800) 520-6455
milkweed.org

Published 2024 by Milkweed Editions
Printed in the United States of America
Cover design by Mary Austin Speaker
Author photo by Cybele Knowles
24 25 26 27 28 5 4 3 2 1
Second Edition

Library of Congress Control Number: 2024930256

Milkweed Editions is committed to ecological stewardship. We strive to align our book production practices with this principle, and to reduce the impact of our operations in the environment. We are a member of the Green Press Initiative, a nonprofit coalition of publishers, manufacturers, and authors working to protect the world's endangered forests and conserve natural resources.

CONTENTS

I.

II.

III.

IV.

V.

I want my time to grant me what time can't grant itself

AL-MUTANABBI

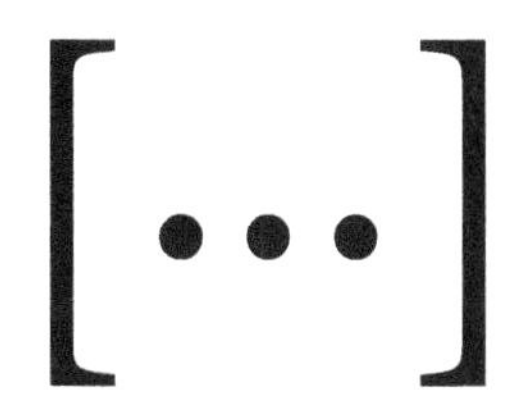

I.

[...]

I am unfinished business.
The business that did not finish me

or my parents
won't leave my children
in peace. In my right hand,

a paper. In my left, a feather.
To toss, to quill, to meet

my terminal velocity.
I forget Palestine

has a kind way of remembering
those who mark it for slaughter,

and those it marks for life.
I write for the future

because my present is demolished.
I fly to the future

to retrieve my demolished present
as a legible past. To see

what isn't hard to see
in a world that doesn't.

[...]

Daily you wake up to the killing of your people, their tongue accented in your mother's milk.

Daily you wake up to the killing of my people. Do you? Censored, the news. Shadow banned. McCarthyed.

I wake up to what I go to bed with. Without dreams. Nightmares are my days into weeks into months. Will you stand with me next year or the next? I will be then as my people now. Wandering the carnage you authorized or protested.

I am removing me from the we of you. Sick leave. Unpaid. Administrative. Long hiatus. I have watched vultures before. Their committees over carcasses they did not kill. Daily the vultures are mute.

Daily my father waits for the rip in his soul to widen. The last of his siblings alive, he dreads mourning a niece, a nephew, their kids, or grandkids.

Daily I remain where they remain. My mother's two oldest sisters, the pocket money they set aside for her schooling during previous wars on their right to exist.

My life, the accent of their accent when my mind goes. Daily, my English is less identifiable to you. I search for a mole on a cheek, on the corner of a lip, a holy stone, a blackness to kiss.

And my shards, collectible, then a collector's piece. The dead are here to teach us what? What do the slain teach? And grief sings being because the dead don't grieve or sing. Not without the living, they don't.

Daily, this pre-ancestral memory, impossible to walk away from, to stay with. It keeps saying that all our names are false.

Daily, your nuance. Your attention to detail, drop by drop. Another round of sedatives. Sedative: the capital. Body: the sweat shop.

[...]

You have entered the tunnel.
There is a light in the endless tunnel.
Every word you think of
has already been written
by you or others who skim
the spume of their seas.
They love to travel.
They love you more when you're dead.
You're more alive to them dead.
Resuscitated, you enter the tunnel
you've been walking toward,
marched toward, expelled into,
dug with your spleen,
the graveyard of your blood.
Your mass, excised,
clears your margins.
The passive voice
is your killer's voice.
From time to time, they vote.
From time to time, language dies.
It is dying now.
Who is alive to speak it?

[...]

Ceasefire now. Before Thanksgiving?
By Christmas or the New Year?

On MLK Day or Easter? Forever?
Before old tricks find themselves out,

and genocide is seen through, this year or the next
decade, and scholars sign off on it.

Repetition won't guarantee wisdom,
but cease now
before your wisdom is an echo.

We need to differentiate
between the dead and the not-here.

We require you to restore your mind
to your heart, its earliest version,

before the world touched it.
After the massacre

who will emerge innocent?
And I, a serf,
online or behind fences.

Ceasefire now. Sure, you will
have to grant more rights,
cede new ground. Sure,

revolution shall not last.
Shall not end.

[...]

Because you are
what you other,
you are to me

as close to the light
as a great contortionist
in a great heist. In time

your joints will fail you.
The light will hit you.
Alarms will go off.

I don't wish that you get caught,
only that you quit
your addiction to secure

the ancient wonder
as yours alone.

Fuck museums.
Wonder belongs to all.

Come out. I've been waiting for you
by one of your escape routes.
They're familiar to me.

Not long ago, I was like you.
Before the light hit me.

Stick Figures

The petals were phone-number tags
of an ad for a roommate

on the bulletin board in the department's hallway.

Then the petals were between yes and no,
the tags were bangs,
bumper stickers, sticky labels,

tear-off strips
for runways and runaways during war.

Everyone loves a winner. I'll be loved by a few.
They will be forgotten as I will be forgotten.

The petals belong to my people, who like any other people
are capable of—
or incapable of—given time,
the great provider.

I sketch horror like children draw stick figures.
I distill the body in mass graves: sticks and bones
break my heart of stone,

a heart of stone pays the mind,
and a heart of water has let the mind go.

According to the testimonies
the trees were leafing
through documents,
the birds had transferred to better schools.

The petals were corpses that made a bridge,
corpses that turned a wadi
red, a river ink.

The petals had names:
ordinary citizen
turned beast,
ordinary citizen period,
majority souls
silent and silenced,
the tree next door
for uprooting
the tree that palms
a scoop from the river,
whales we nudge
to suicide, a willow
sounding the barrier
reef: Say when
will the madness end?

I asked the petals, but they were between yes and no.
That's where the children headed,
between yes and no, to do the asking themselves.

The petals answered or kept to themselves.
The petals spoke only to bees and such.
They spoke to us, the children clarified, through bees and such.

And what did the bees and such hear?
We did not have their ears, the kids replied

but there were also ants around, they said.
The ants told the worms
to tell the birds to bounce back.

The petals were starlings, grackles in a football field
on a middle school morning shelter. The fog told the grackles
the worms were looking for roommates.

The petals ate the worms.
The tags wore big toes
in rows of yes and rows of no.

The petals kept my toes warm.

[...]

They did not mean to kill the children.
They meant to.
Too many kids got in the way
of precisely imprecise
one-ton bombs
dropped a thousand and one times
over the children's nights.
They will not forgive the children this sin.
They wanted to save them from future sins.
Or send them wrapped lifetimes
of reconstructive
surgical hours pro bono,
mental anguish to pass down
to their offspring.
Will the children have offspring?
This is what the bomb-droppers
did not know they wanted:
to see if others will be like them
after unquantifiable suffering.
They wanted to lead
their own study, but forgot
that not all suffering worships power
after survival. What childhood does
a destroyed childhood beget?
My parents showed me the way.

Mimesis

This morning, I don't know how,
an inch-long baby frog

entered my house
during the extermination

of human animals live on TV.
I recognized the baby's dread.

It leapt into shadows,
under the couch, into my shoe.

My son was watching.
Gently, patiently
I followed it
on my knees

with shattered heart
and plastic bag.

Coaxed it, caught it,
released it
into the yard,
and started to cry.

Bonsai Weeping Willow

My dog contracted diabetes and left me
stuck with the bill. A lover boy

he never met a person he didn't like
or a food he didn't taste.

A lucky dog, he can't attain enlightenment,
but no heaven without hell.

In the next life he'll come back
as a person who can't afford their insulin.

I've met many of those. One buried
the little of it she rationed
in the damp fertile ground

so that it would keep.
Another was comatose,

a soldier in an army that didn't care.
What is an army that cares?

[...]

Your grandeur is your insignificance.

The patience that takes your heart out
into the wilderness, the impatience
that undresses you in a crowd.

This is what faith taught you:
this way art, that way God, this way
hierarchy dissolves.

Your grandeur is your insignificance.

And the whole world
in an atom in the mind,
the atom compounding,
transmitting a world.

It's not as easy as it used to be
to be alone with the earth.

Garden, I choose you.
You are the time
I want to lose.

[...]

Plumb line. For the longest time
I heard it as plum line.
I adore a perfect fruit   its flawless groove
revealing division, remaining one.
            Your earth is lead
that poisons the stream of my memory.
Your phosphorus plumbs me to the bone.
I know how it came to this. How did it?
More than words, you speak in silences
that amplify white spaces
in which white is not water.
It smells. I can taste it. And water is life,
closer to life than dirt and stone.
            Dirt and stone,
is that what you love most to taste? I spin and raise
my taste and smell into a love like water.
How will I go on living
with orchestras that conduct my thirst?
It's been done before.
There are precedents, always will be,
and there will be Gaza after the dark times.
There will be gauze. And we will all stand
indicted for not standing against the word
and our studies of the word
that dissect what ceases to be water.
Why do you crave plumbing the depths of dust so?
Dust and ashes, I'm ahead of my time,
my time is only mine when you're in it
            with an open heart.
An open heart has two ears, two eyes.
One set for breath, one for blood. And the dance
between them, grooved

like a plum. I will survive. There is no better song.
My body knows my memory
is my keeper beyond the loss
in which you're hooked on naming.
        Can you be water?
        One day you will be
that kind of divine.

[...]

Then my friend in Nablus had a dream.
The sun rose from the west

while he was praying
on a marble floor on fire.

Everyone one was fleeing,
but he kept with his prayers,

felt only peace.
Then peace began to shake.
He was bound up in an iron cage

and tied to an animal
outside the cage. What animal?
It was no beast of burden.

And the beast yanked him
repeatedly into the bars
trying to get him out to no avail.

Did the animal want to free
my friend or eat him?
He wasn't sure.

He was bloodied, bruised,
and it was November.
It was dawn, and time to pray.

[...]

And out of nowhere a girl receives an ovation

from her rescuers,
all men
on their knees and bellies

clearing the man-made rubble
with their bare hands,
disfigured by dust
into ghosts.

All disasters are natural
including this one
because humans are natural.

The rescuers tell her
she's incredible, powerful,
and for a split second, before the weight

of her family's disappearance
sinks her, she smiles,

like a child
who lived for seven years above ground
receiving praise.

Progress Notes

Our progress wants to travel back to our beginning
alone. To find us

with lances and no last names.
My issue with the Anthropocene

is that I can't get my dog to change
his drishti during his downward pose:
from snout forward
to gaze back between his hind legs.
And then all this marine

life we cleanse. Sushi, be gone.
Empires, fall down to your knees
with your fillets and bycatches.

To be vegetarian is not enough.
Grow your own shit. Be satisfied
with quitting your job. After each discovery,
expansionist desire is countered
with lust for the microscale.

The micro grows a monster, a master.
Didn't we come upon ourselves by chance,
a bone sticking out
of a million years?
Why won't we open our chests and drop them like weapons
for cosmic waves to wash us down?

Losses have been heavy.
Losses will be heavy.
And prophets are environmentalists, revolutionaries,
civil rights activists, and meditative beams.

They always have been.
They tried. They try again.

[...]

As boys we played a game
called Fisherman:

You built a pyramid
of empty soda cans

for your foes to knock down
with a tennis ball,
always yellow.

Then gathered into a field as fish.
For the pyramid as for the fishing

the ball was the spear.
If you could cleanly catch it
and fling it far, make your rivals

scramble to reclaim their weapon,
without which they were nothing,

while you rebuilt what you could
of what they destroyed

before the spear reentered the fray.
Oh, the thuds stung and were mean.

One by one we'd fall.

To make the pyramid whole again
meant you were not wiped out.

And your team won.

[...]

America, where those who pass,
pass through the needle's eye,
and on the other side

my son asks
if I am a product
of her dream.

Has the self
ever been the subject
of so much propaganda?

Who is without echo?
An empire of nobodies
floods the market,

they come bearing
a fleet of arks.

[...]

"Your oppressor," they said,
"has suffered more than you have."

"As have others," you said,
"who are yet to hurt me but can't

quit pondering how
I might have harmed them in my sleep,
might harm them still."

"Your oppressor," they said, "shines
much light on the world."

"But the light of the world," you said,
"isn't the light of the heart."

"You're among the lucky ones," they said.
"Your oppressor's heart is your host.
And it recruits."

"But I'll have to wait my turn," you said,
"before my story, held hostage, is released."

"Why the hurry?" they asked, "and to whom
do you think your wounds
would be criteria

in a democracy
of loneliness worse than death?"

"A feedback loop," you said,
"exporting lesions to the brain."

"And the brain is one," they said,
"because the lord is one."

So much music out there.

[...]

Hope left me
but it isn't true.

Malady stayed by my side.
We grew intimate.
Whatever night chased me

I chased it with night.
I grew ignorant in love,

I grew an ignorant love.
From state to state

allies and friends helped me
to shrink my malady

into a corner.
It whined.
And on occasion
accused me of betrayal.

It had the right.
Sometimes I let it nurse me.

[...]

Why don't you denounce
what you ask me to denounce.
We can do it together on the count of three.
Or you should go first

on account of your obsession
with my going first, your grand inquisitor role
isn't for doves, your better angel
is calling you

to let go
of holding on and to hold on
to letting go: Your misguided vengeance,
your unequaled pain,
why on my body?
What about the body you can't beat up?
Why anybody

including you?
Listen, what you can't smell
is the taste of all things that come to pass
which are all things.
Listen, ears
are erogenous.
I'll lick your ears against revenge.

[...]

The fireflies you kept in a jar as a child
until their light went out.

It was only that one time.

Your light is not for jarring.
Your light is now for jarring.

Your captors translate
your anguish into a return

on investment. To be
good again. For all to see.

They house your voice in glass.

Eid Mubarak

Our past wants to live on
longer than the past that preceded it.
The latter had mostly enigmas, menhirs, mud-house
phantoms, papyrus, and what we have is far
more difficult to imagine
time obliterating. As though

only our present contains the things
that dilate into ordinary miracles:
synaptic uptake, electronic pleats
between history and stars,
coronaries that dethrone their hearts.

What else is inside
the air we are inside
and pull inside us?
The air that carries.

If we disappear, we will not disappear
in the same manner that disappeared those before us.
We will come close to Armageddon but forgive God.
We will interview the dying,

archive them from beyond the grave. Another chance
to make strangers ours: to enter us
as day enters night.

[...]

Long ago we were lovers. Recently
your father died. Your heartache

took you to the desert
where my people are colonized by yours
or an extension thereof.

You visit only as tourist, a donor to
the status quo.
At the height of the meditation retreat,

anyone can feel free of all identity
that isn't born of their making.

Your husband is enlisted.
My people are not without blame,

no people are. Degrees matter.
The boots on necks matter. In the desert,

next to a Bedouin woman who served you
tea from her shack, you sent me a photo

of your first smile in six months.
After your departure,
she will be removed from her dwelling.

In the desert, you renounce all belonging
like someone who has so much of it.

The surplus you keep for yourself.

[...]

What if I still love you? If I don't love you anymore.
Without malice or rancor.

What would it take for you to speak with me again?
There is air, there is no air to clear.

I don't want to die here.

What if you let me trace your skin,
the skin that hides your outside

and lines your within.
What if you hate my guts

since my not-so-nice-albeit-precise diagnosis
wasn't delivered how you wanted to hear.

What if, now that I am not the person I was
before I knew you were in the world,

a love capable of being two.

And your song for me is not mine for you,
if you have a song left for me at all.

Without rancor or malice.
Why speak again?

[...]

Or we break out
by becoming seeds
that rise once every 17 years

miming cicada clicking
their brass and horn,
devouring silence

in six days and seven nights,
with or without touching
the Joseph of our dreams,

the founder of our state
          of perishing beauty.

In Arabic, pain is an anagram of hope.
In Arabic, dream is clemency's twin.
In Arabic, Joseph holds love

like a jug of wine.
And everyone's forgiven.

[...]

Not everyone
is a physician

but sooner or later everyone
fails to heal.

In Gaza, a girl and her brother
rescued their fish
from the rubble of airstrikes. A miracle

its tiny bowl
didn't shatter.

II.

[...]

Aggressors also grieve.

What hell a lucky life can be.

I tried but couldn't

catch fish in a mirage,

headed straight to the sea.

The sea fished out like a land.

My other half-lives

did not set me free. The mirage

of the solid self in ruins,

gigantic in departure. And the waves

of the sea growing serene whisper

what they used to scream:

I am not your translator.

I Seem As If I Am: Ten Maqams

1.

I'm not a war but someone is

saying my mind,
canonized and colonized, is out of sync with the freedom of your body.

I'm an old war   that your world isn't in love with anymore.

The players are well known. No one agrees
on what constitutes them:

justice, ineffable suffering, the right to defend
the right to eradicate. I refuse

what the war wants: that the path I seek in peace be sought through war.

2.

Your liver is on fire. It's not
because of drink
that your liver is on fire.

Your soul is in your enemy's fist,
and he won't release it.

Deep inside the captivity, a parched partridge
rests in your heart. Now and again she remembers

a brook, flaps her wings, kicks off with her legs, claws.

A free heart within a caged chest is free.

3.

Wars come and wars go
          and sometimes I cry
because the dam breaks.

Arbitrarily, you say, the dam breaks.
Arbitrary as a straw,

the camel grows
another hump,
and I grow wealthy like a flood,

rush sea and plain,
the sea spits me back,
the plains muddy me

then disappear me.

What is joy? I was told it can be a family
that held on to their father's corpse against the flood
so it wouldn't wash away.

4.

A small collective is no less capable than a large one.

Is there a prize the empire hasn't won?

Whitman was a prostitute in the way Benjamin said Baudelaire

had said that the task of the modern poet is to prostitute themselves.

Emily Dickinson didn't. Maybe a tiff. And janitors

are unacknowledged legislators of their proverbs, their poncif.

Thus the eagle will come back for your liver. We have time.

Tickle me until I beg you to stop. Liver is our safe word.

Laughter as torture, a shortcut to insanity.

More so than sorrow is.

Sorrow the turtle.

5.

It’s 12:42 p.m. where love is sold in markets
that make love for other wars. My city

market translates: At a traffic light an old man hands me a rose and says,
It’s for nothing. He meant, I don’t have to pay nothing

or sign a petition.
How our faces appear to him. Quickly
he walks away to let the weight

of the rose grow sovereign in my heart

to the extent it can
on the eve of a new war.

6.

When did the new war begin?

Whoever gets to write it most
gets to erase it best.

The new war has been coming for a long time.
The old war has been going for a long time.

Coming to a body near me, and going on my body.

The combatants,
I've heard them call out to their mothers, seen them
do as they were told.

And the civilians
offer compassion to the combatants,
like food for war.

The bad news is that your old war is the growth in your life.
        The good news

is that it's eligible for renewal online. After love

has reached the speed of light
it is invisible again.

7.

To Al-Buhturi—another man
from outside Aleppo
who found himself on the outskirts of Baghdad

more centuries ago
than the fingers on a pair of hands handing away roses
at a traffic light on the eve of a new war.

The war you're thinking of, I made
you think of, is a red herring.

Buhturi tells us a story we don't believe.
He encountered a hungry wolf, which he killed then grilled.
He was corresponding with the barbarism of man.

This, in contrast to an earlier Arab poet who,
by brandishing his sword to the wolf,
established a memorandum of understanding

with the beast. Across fire and smoke
they shared a meal from his sack.
A bite for me, a bite for you.

Each poet singular, a snowflake
of meaning, of nonsense.

Toward the end of his poem, Buhturi dispensed with the wolf
that was and the one that wasn't.
Human and nonhuman memories merge:

> "Nights may rule unjustly over us, unintended
> is the ruling of the daughters of time."

8.

Why daughters? It may be a creation myth or prosody
that determined the gender of time's offspring.

He also said:

> "Disasters follow one another,
> the far ones grow near, the near ones, far.
> All destruction runs
> its business to the ground."

We lead the world in saving what we destroy.
We've learned to see how predators see.

Though we are never full. We are
always some kind of content, seldom content.

I want to learn how colors choose flowers, not how we.

9.

Who knows
more than the other about themselves and the other:
Love or life?

Life says: I will make you to make love.
Love says: I make life so that I am.

10.

He also said:

> "After demolition, a comet
> may leave water behind."

There are more flowers that aren't
over graves than over them.

The same for grass and grains of sand.
Does grass grow toward your tiny heart?

Love. Life. Language.
Life. Love. Language.
Language. Life. Love.

Musical chairs.

The love I wanted to be, I wanted to be
the questions my heart no longer asks.

The language I wanted to be, I will be
after I'm done talking.

The life I wanted to live
as one and not only.

Maqam for a Green Silence

A 93-year-old woman in the throes of her final yet protracted delirium in a hospital bed turned to me and said, "Come here, what are you afraid of?" She was a Rumi and Shakespeare scholar. I had been visiting her daily, one of her children constantly in the room. I didn't know the answer. All this time I had been busy fearing and not seeing what it is I feared, since what we fear changes with time, even if all fear can be reduced to one thing, a thing yoked to life. Perhaps she thought I was one of her children and she was encouraging me to let her go, which, as a doctor, I was working on. What did Rumi or Shakespeare say to her that morning? Over the next few days, I asked my friends her question. Two mothers said that outliving their kids was their biggest fear. Their answer was immediate, as if the speed of the reply reflected the clarity of the heart. One of them said it first—a breath before the other. According to legend, she who spoke it first will outlive the other by at least one exhalation. A father, I felt shame that this reply was not instant to me, though I had tasted the shadow of this incomprehensible grief, which, if survived, is never cured. The mother who will live longer turned to me and asked, "What about you, what's your biggest fear?" I said that silence was. "What do you mean by silence?" I shrugged. Then I asked another father. "This is the mother of all questions," he said.

I thought of Moses's mother. Her heart. And of Moses when, on God's command, he sought a saint who lives beyond time and place, whose name derives from the color green. God wanted Moses to experience other obstacles of faith. Al-Khidr's only condition for the prophet to join him on his journey was Moses's unconditional silence. Moses said he was up for it, and the saint said, "You won't be able to bear it." Incapable of green silence, Moses broke his promise three times—as the saint sank a ship and its crew, demolished a crumbling wall he could have restored for a beleaguered people, and then killed a child. Fed up with the prophet's objections, the saint sent Moses away. That he who knows more than another will also know less.

III.

[...]

Some emotion reappraises me.
In the here and now I sent myself

into, I am not who I wished
to be in the afterworld.

When will I smile again? What tourism
will help me to
what body?

Kufic

I say swan dance,
you say phoenix moth.

*

A sublime distance from the sun,
we made a species of each alphabet.

*

Destruction a toy
monster I open
my mouth.

*

It's unbearable
to want so much
the thing whose ending
you're likely to pray for one day.

*

Endless love. Who wants that?
And who doesn't? Even cells
touch each other to say goodbye.

*

And you pray for a kind ending.

*

A man dreams
of a dead beloved.
A woman dreams of a man
who doesn't dream of a dead beloved.

*

Fireflies glowing.
Bats feeding.
Texture of darkness.

[...]

I spot a sycamore and register it.
I smell white coffee blossoms
and vibrate in the breeze.

Whatever the disposition of my senses,
I make into a map, network my feelings,
spectacular yet pedestrian

until you appear. I start travelling
toward unravelling,
but no prior belief in the foretold

eases what details decoy:
your name is new
or spelled differently,
all your features, too.

You show me a snapdragon,
I tongue a fishmouth.
Your face engorges light, the dark
dots my body

and says that
since time has become my essence
it will lay me to waste.
You can say this

is pain talking to evolve a fear. You can ask
how many fears before any will do.

I glimpsed a door and darted through it.
A light wind touched a bloom.
It clothed then unclothed
a permission to be lonely with you.

Barzakh

We used to swim in it.
We swam only once.

*

Your window overlooked the sea.
Whenever we prayed

to anchovies and sardines,
your grandmother cooked.

*

Great joys exhaust me,
small ones bring me to tears.

A thief, I am not
guilty, I mugged
some of your beautiful years.

*

We used to swim in it.

Our bodies are not what they were
to ourselves or to the other.

We built a temple over
why we had built it.

*

Each morning I clasp
your bracelet, your necklace.

Your earlobes, two buoys
on the tip of my tongue.

*

Generously you dance
so that love is fair.
Alone you sing
as though no one listening would dare.

*

The sea
we swam in
and the sea we're yet to
transfigure.

Leaves, Glass

Autumn eggshells
toward a gazelle

who doesn't care if she's being watched
so long as no sound startles.

All I want is to revolve around you
seeking you front and back.

Not as a prophet. Physics
was never my strong suit.

During childhood
God was clouds

that settled only themselves.
All was none and none was all.

We harnessed electricity
to scramble our contemplation of light.

From the heart to the mind
is much easier than the mind

to the heart. Apropos all that,
have you seen two snails mate?

They elongate out of their spirals,
and if the occasion requires it, change their sex.

It's summer. We're here.
It's humid. The grass is wet.

Maqam for Apricot

How old were you when the foot thing started?
With your toe knuckles
stroking the sole of your other foot,

your fingertips meridians for your breast,
as you touch yourself,
as I touch you.

I tried to watch. You stopped.
Is your body still teaching you things?
I learned to fan my toes

and say something about my body
without you next to it.
The doctor in me is drowning in mirrors.

I feel the world
as we feel each other. Cold,
tender, cruel. Feather, scalpel, gauze.
Pill, whip, chakra.

We ambulate, we ambulance.
We bear weight and bait
our breath to bare our death.
Orchid, snow, titmouse. Four

the seasons and four
the rooms in the heart.

Your feet
and my small
soft hands.

[...]

In the arboretum the mosquitoes were polite.
They purchased our blood for a fair price
as we paused for the flowers.

My iPhone identified the plants.
Delete, reinstall. The truth

rides photons, always arriving
beautiful, like God, periodically dead or terminated.

Hibiscus. Marigold. My intelligence
offers my ignorance hope,
my wish manacles me to it.

We needed memory, we got myelin.
Slow at first to guard us

from the animal we're destined to suppress,
rise above—and then fast,

foaming at the terabyte.
Between loss and gain, we discard and preserve.

Look how we put on clothes into the grave.
How others don't.

Ode to an Onion

You're a planet
and the soil your space.

Your green poles tickle the sun,
your tubes and antennas sense events

for Ramses's eyes in the underworld,
and also in Ashkelon,

before Salaheddin
burnt it to the ground
to jerk the heart of Monsieur Lionheart awake.

Your people left
but you stuck around
your many sisters.

I simply love you
as I cry and dismember you,
and most of all

you're sweet.
A caramel mount in olive oil,
God has not forsaken you.

For years I laid siege to your sting
to nurture more of your sugars.
I give up. I miss you as you are,

sulfur-heavy,
a throne for water.

No Kissing, No Biting

A heart with nostrils   I keep submerged
and risk snuffing the part of my muscle you had settled,

from which you needed to be smoked out,
like a bee, I hope.

Will you keep the honey?

In the last six months, I wrote you 37 letters,
211 in the past two years in batches of ten,
the first of them not much different from the last,

the reason I sent none.
In next week's memo I intend to explain:

Since the chest pain you once caused me
has ended, your gifts to me have doubled.
For example, I have noticed the distances

those things I hold so near inside me
slip out into. I shouldn't have to tell which
one you are.

This Time, Actual Bees

The beehive in the front yard, inverted domes
in our water meter hole, a random event.

The bees would not miss us if the entire neighborhood went missing.
The reverse isn't true. The mind goes to self

as the self comes to mind.
The mind tells the self, I made you,
and the self asks, who gave you that idea?

The bears might notice. The clover fields and horses.
The beekeeper cost a good penny, smoked the bees

out of their minds, removed the hive live,
showed me the queen,
guarantor of posterity.

Soon the bees recovered their senses,
reentered their cabins, most of their cells intact.

And what do you do with the honey? I asked.
It's for their wintering, she said.

IV.

[...]

You who remove me from my house
are blind to your past
which never leaves you,
blind to what's being done
to me now by you.
Now, dilatory, attritional,
so that the crime
is climate change and not a massacre,
so that the present never ends.
But I'm closer to you
than you are to yourself,
and this, my enemy friend,
is the definition of distance.
Oh don't be indignant.
Watch the video. I'll send you the link
in which you cleanse me item after limb
thrown into the street to march where
my catastrophe in the present
is still not the size of your past:
Is this the wall
you throw your dice against?
I'm speaking etymologically. I'm okay
with the scales tipping your way,
I'm not into that. I have a heart that rots,
resists, and hopes. I have genes,
like yours, that don't subscribe
to the damage pyramid.
You who remove me from my house
have also evicted my parents
and their parents from theirs:

How is the view from my window?
How does my salt taste?
Shall I condemn myself a little
for you to forgive yourself
in my body? Oh how you love
my body, my house.

[...]

I can't explain it. Something about pattern
turning into rhythm. All my life
I knew liberty would be mine
after great disaster is visited upon me.

Though some attain it
after visiting disasters on others,
it isn't liberty they attain.

What is disaster? And what liberty? Years later,
I came across a book about a boy
whose fears lived in everything he lived.

Without reading the book, I had read it.
I was not that boy. I was the fear
he wanted to be real, the right part

for another's wrong life. The helping hand
his fantasy craved. Kicking and screaming

my freedom came. Freedom that had been lost
and won back, not always in the same place, but always
the same freedom. Carried on shoulders,

crawling out of the ground, falling from the air,
onto the shore, into the self, etc.

Devastated, the boy was satisfied.
We're all the same kind of animal.

Hummingbird

Who here has not loved
like no one else in the world has
before them or since?

Your blood wondering what more
it can open up in your skin,
all the light rushing in like a fool

through the tiniest holes,
the invisible pores.

And then love ended.
You returned to yourself.

Who here has not lived
the passing

of all thinking
through the language of love?

[...]

You will be when we be. You will stay when we stay.
You've made our tears yours, your memory
no longer possible without us.

You will need our sky for yours to hold up,
and our sea will teach you return.

We will return
though not
as you have.

Say you're sorry. Will you
say sorry once? How long before your first remorse?

We absolve you of reparation, promise you forgiveness.
How long before you enter us to leave yourself?

In the fabric of origin, there was a loophole, and we a camel
that went through. One hump or two, what's the difference?
Weren't you once a camel, too?

Our bodies are real. Our ghosts are here.
Where did you leave your ghosts?

They would have taught you kindness
and ordinary mourning.
They would have led you past precedent.

You will miss what you vanish.
You will be when we be.

Dedication

To those whose memory, imagination, and bodies are my memory, imagination, and body. From the collective to the one under the same assault, no matter our location on Earth. "Our bodies have different ways of knowing, but our bodies know." To the martyrs who witness from above, and the living who witness on the ground. To those who will be killed on the last day of the war. To those who will be killed on the first day after the war ends. To those who succumb in the humanitarian window of horror. An hour before the pause, a minute after. To those who die of a broken heart during and after the war. To those who gather their families to die together so that no survivor suffers survival alone. To those who scatter their families so that they're not all wiped out from the civil record. To the babies whose death certificates marked their brief presence on earth before their birth certificates could be issued: they were not given names. To the elderly who endured 1948 and lived to see their descendants erased. To the young born under the sign of siege and are the only members of their families left: Will you stand up and form a small nation? To those who died because dialysis was no longer possible, no water, electricity, and fuel: you were murdered. To those who will develop kidney stones and liver failure from unclean water. To diarrhea, cold, and flu. To those who are maimed and will search for their missing limbs underground, across borders, and won't find their extremities after they find them. To those whose cherubic hearts couldn't handle the shock, and to those whose nicotine hearts blocked the flow: you, too, were killed. To those who were killed because they refused to leave their homes to live in tents. To those who were killed on their way to the tents. To those who were killed in their tents with the cats they sheltered. To those who were killed in UN shelters and in schools. To those who were killed because they were medics, nurses, doctors, teachers, coders and decoders, and the last honest journalists. To those who thought their biggest fear was to outlive their children. To those who are free of the fear of death, because tyranny spoke its final answer, and it was total. To those in a concentration camp the size of a metropolis: the only life they knew. To Jerusalem and Jenin. To Jenin and Jerusalem. To the children who played in the craters the bombs made, if the sand was right. The bodies we count are not the bodies we retrieve from the river to the sea. And the bodies we retrieve are not always identifiable. To those who guard their dead from the starving dogs of war who are different from the dogs of war that starved them. To those who cannot guard the corpses from rats. To those who rummage through the rubble for clothes, gloves, forks, plates, soap, toothpaste, and wooden furniture to burn for cooking and to keep warm. They will not accept your apology after the genocide, "O theology of empire." To diapers, scissors, sanitary pads, to shoes, prenatal care, and onesies. To beards and headscarves. To erased archives that housed centuries. To pulverized libraries. To Saint Porphyrius and the Omari Mosque. And to those who hold vigils, day and night, for a hand sticking out of a crack in the wreckage. "Wave to us, can you wave to us?" they say. And she does. And it buoys them from the river to the sea. To those who never heard her voice and loved her in silence. To those who cried over the animals they left behind: some cows, some goats, many chickens and ducks, and to the ducks and chickens that starving dogs did not spare. To the roosters crowing over the rhythmic blasts. To starlings, sparrows, seabirds, sardine, and mullet. To mules and donkeys dying of a thousand cuts: Who's whispering in your ears? To the horses led from stable rubble to rubble stable. To palm trees, zaatar, basil, and tomatoes that weapons poisoned. To palm trees: the natural reserve for the phoenix ashes. To olive oil: preserver of time. To natural gas reserves, may you be a stake through the heart of vampires. To flour, bread, and bakeries. To those who did not fulfill American media's requests to boil the ocean: those who couldn't celebrate their birthdays with cake and candles during the massacre. To the martyrs who did not furnish their photos for their killers to air them on their compassionate TV. To the martyrs who did not speak English. To the relatable and unrelatable, the translatable and untranslatable Palestinian flesh. To those who recite the verse of return. To those whose minds have shattered into shrapnel nothing can remove from their souls. To those with dementia: may it save you from the full scale of terror. To forgetfulness when a mercy. To remembrance when a mercy. To crutches and wheelchairs. To those who composed songs and sang them to the syncopated thuds of annihilation. To life. To light. The light is dead, long live the light. To those who prayed in the pitch-black night to the power of God, the only power available to them, but could not meditate on moon and stars. To those who found a way to fall in love, make love, construct a romance, a secret rendezvous, hold a wedding, and dream of moon and stars. To those who insist on homing their pigeons during the war. Have your pigeons come home? To those, to those, to those. We are not afraid of love from the river to the sea.

V.

Sunbird

I flit
from gleaming river
to glistening sea.

From all that we
to all that me.

Fresh east to salty west,
southern sweet

and northern free.
There is a lake

between us.
And aquifers
for cactus

and basins
of anemone
from the river

to the sea.
From womb
to breath, and one
with oneness

I be:
from the river
to the sea.

Acknowledgments

Thanks to the editors of the following publications in which some of these poems appeared in earlier versions: *Adi Magazine*, *ArabLit Quarterly*, *Harper's Magazine*, *Jewish Currents*, Lit Hub, *Los Angeles Review of Books*, *New York Times Magazine*, Poets.org, *The Nation*, *The Rumpus*, *Visible Binary*, *Washington Post*, and *Yale Review*.

FADY JOUDAH has published six collections of poems: *The Earth in the Attic*; *Alight*; *Textu*, a book-long sequence of short poems whose meter is based on cellphone character count; *Footnotes in the Order of Disappearance*; and, most recently, *Tethered to Stars*. He has translated several collections of poetry from the Arabic and is the co-editor and co-founder of the Etel Adnan Poetry Prize. He was a winner of the Yale Series of Younger Poets competition in 2007 and has received a PEN award, a Banipal/Times Literary Supplement prize from the UK, the Griffin Poetry Prize, a Guggenheim Fellowship, the Arab American Book Award, and the Jackson Poetry Prize. He lives in Houston, with his wife and kids, where he practices internal medicine.

Founded as a nonprofit organization in 1980, Milkweed Editions is an independent publisher. Our mission is to identify, nurture, and publish transformative literature, and build an engaged community around it.

Milkweed Editions is based in Bdé Óta Othúŋwe (Minneapolis) within Mní Sota Makhóčhe, the traditional homeland of the Dakhóta people. Residing here since time immemorial, Dakhóta people still call Mní Sota Makhóčhe home, with four federally recognized Dakhóta nations and many more Dakhóta people residing in what is now the state of Minnesota. Due to continued legacies of colonization, genocide, and forced removal, generations of Dakhóta people remain disenfranchised from their traditional homeland. Presently, Mní Sota Makhóčhe has become a refuge and home for many Indigenous nations and peoples, including seven federally recognized Ojibwe nations. We humbly encourage our readers to reflect upon the historical legacies held in the lands they occupy.

milkweed.org

Milkweed Editions, an independent nonprofit literary publisher, gratefully acknowledges sustaining support from our board of directors, the McKnight Foundation, the National Endowment for the Arts, and many generous contributions from foundations, corporations, and thousands of individuals—our readers. This activity is made possible by the voters of Minnesota through a Minnesota State Arts Board Operating Support grant, thanks to a legislative appropriation from the arts and cultural heritage fund.

Interior design by Mary Austin Speaker
Typeset in Bely

Bely was designed by Roxane Gataud for the TypeTogether foundry in 2014. Bely is designed with classical proportions for maximum legibility and received the Type Directors Club Award of Excellence in Type Design in 2017.

Printed in the USA
CPSIA information can be obtained
at www.ICGtesting.com
JSHW022031010724
65693JS00004B/116